SHINING STAR

LIZA LAHA

XpressPublishing
An imprint of Notion Press

XpressPublishing
An imprint of Notion Press

Old No. 38, New No. 6
McNichols Road, Chetpet
Chennai - 600 031

First Published by Notion Press 2019
Copyright © LIZA LAHA 2019
All Rights Reserved.

ISBN 978-1-64661-941-2

Contents

Contents

When You Are Calm Internally The Entire External Environment Automatically Becomes Calm."

Foreword

This book is written to lighten the path of the youth. It also serves to answer the complicated questions of present world showcasing its solutions. This book is mostly written for the growing generation to help them understand the purpose of their life and provide them with a basic understanding of it. The writings will enhance their thoughts providing them with many innovative aspects of knowledge.

The book reflects on various aspects of the society and expects to create a dream society.

Hope the readers will enjoy this small voyage to the fullest.

Acknowledgements

A sincere gratitude to Shama Prasad Chawdhary, senior teacher of St. Joseph's Convent High School Mosaboni.

CHAPTER ONE

B.E.D. (Bachelor of Emotional Destination) "Soul is composed of emotions. If emotions are ending, soul is depleting."

Every material object is bound with emotions. It is adage to a great extent. The tears rolling down our eyes are pearls of feeling. And, losing even a drop of it cost hard at cash. We are connected to our parents, friends and other loved ones through the one and only glue of emotions. The bride is beautified by a specified make-up artist because she wants to drive all eyes towards her as she is deeply emotionally attached to the auspicious occasion that will initiate her new life.

We are furnished with heaps of present on our golden marriage anniversary, as there are lot of momentous memories that revive the love and spirit of years before. The swimmer spares all her zest and days to embrace the dreamt golden medal to flourish in the world of swimming, her ultimate goal. The baby cries being left alone as it starves for the warmth of his mother's lap. Children are envious for the same latest mobile that is available to his friends.

The soul inside our mortal bodies is immortal because it is composed of various feelings, be it abhor, adore, sympathy, piety, anger, abominable or any other such abstracts. God cannot be seen, we can envision Him only with the acuity of thoughts. Filling our heart with emotions will pay not-ending cheerfulness. Emotions are highly worthy and so it needs to move in a lighted path. It should neither be misused nor should it be misguided. High–level emotions are not destined to everyone.

One is filled with pure emotions when we reach the rank of spirituality. One is filled with impure emotions when we are accursed for wrongs. Now the questions are how to distinguish between pure and impure emotions? Which one is the right one to acquire and how to do that? What are the immediate pros and corns of it will be? What will be its objectives? What are the programs to carry out the objectives? What cost is to be paid for the gain of it? All these have been briefly described following:

PURE EMOTION

IMPURE EMOTION

①*The emotion that exits for emotion sake only is described as pure emotion.*

①*The emotion that has many other motives enjoined with it is called impure emotion.*

②*It is a plotted design by heart.*

②*It is a plotted plan by heart and mind.*

③*It is immortal.*

③*It is mortal.*

④*It guaranties a sweet pain.*

④*It guaranties bitter relief.*

⑤*It stands also for sacrifice.*

⑤*It asks for sacrifice.*

⑥*It is to feel.*

⑥*It is to understand.*

Talking of the first difference, pure emotion has the only purpose to feel and execute it for its execution. Very different to this is our impure emotions that's execution is more than fifty percent dependent on some mixed motive.

Then, is the second difference that speaks of its origination. Pure emotions are termed to be 'pure' because of its origin, that is, from a purely pure location; from our heart. Here they are the monks and abbess of the heart leading it possibly to a semester. On the other hand is the impure emotions, since they originate from our mind; a place where all ace and abysmal feelings are fused together, nothing his found in a pure state here and so it is termed as 'impure' emotions. And they act as the abbess and monks of the head leading it possibly to a disaster.

Inspired by the lines in the poetry- A Psalm of Life by Henry Wadsworth Longfellow is the third difference that clearly mentions lifespan of the emotions. Our body is subjected to decay after we die but this rule is not liable to the soul which is the sole content of our heart. Our souls are immortal least we make them quickly mortal by mixing it with all rubbishes. The purity is never lost by any natural element unless it is affected by outside source of some kind. And so the emotion whose origination is from the heart is imperishable for ages and ages.

And to talk about the impure emotions, they are no different in their origination but only in nature. The theory is absolutely true that emotion comes from our heart only. Those which have the capacity to remain and live in our heart despite extreme pains are a part of heart. And those emotions, which are too weak to take problems as challenges are transferred to our mind where most of them mostly get rotten due to unfavourable conditions in particular. They fail to put up with the unsuitable environment and perish by the quickest time.

The fourth distinction says about what intermediate feelings we will go through. Under purity of emotions we are sure to experience a pain; the most painful one but very ironically, a very sweet pain. It means that the journey of pure emotions is never easy, it will have to cross many needles but its essence of purity spreads over a wide area thus seasoning the pains with its sweetness. I say it as an intermediate feeling because lastly purity ends up purifying all pollutions from our destiny and destining us to a happy feeling.

On the extreme end impure emotions stands, they are sparingly straight forward. Impure emotions certainly grants effective relief to the sharpness of the situation just like how after the medication of high doses we are quickly relieved of the pain but it internally behaves as slow poison causing immense biological damage further. Due to their strong power they kill certain things that are being essential for the functioning of our body but due to some disturbance are badly affected instead of reviving their healing nature.

The next distinction relates to sacrifice. Let us see impure emotions in this case first. It is already said here that they ask for sacrifice. It is very normal to hear knowing the very fact of emotions that any emotion needs the oiling of sacrifice for its smooth running. And so are the impure emotion, even being impure they still retain the characteristics of the need for sacrifice. Pure emotion to say, due to the very nature of emotion it needs sacrifice but it's one feature that differs it from the huge crowd is that it not only asks for sacrifice but also stands for a sacrifice done.

For centuries of human existence have failed to prove the feeling of felling through mind and not heart, that is, despite all controversies it is believed 'the mind is made to think and the heart is meant for emotions'. No invention or teaching has been able to jump across this arena of philosophy. Everyone's view has been adjusted to this understanding. So, on the basis of this understanding for centuries the pure emotion and impure emotion based on their origination from heart and mind is to feel and to understand respectively.

There is another conditioning philosophy that 'nothing is good or bad, it is only based upon the situation we chose the option'. So are the emotions. If the correct emotion is put to use in the correct time then the pros will cover up the corns. The immediate objective of the emotion applied is to connect or disconnect ourselves to a particular thing or person. And the ultimate program to attain the objective is having the guts to apply it correctly at the correct time on correct person or thing. We pay the automatic cost by feeling the sweet pain of pure emotion and bitter relief of impure emotion.

<u>Designing your emotions</u>

Emotions make a man a 'perfect man'. It is no less in value than the most precious objects. Nowadays there is a menacing problem that people face; depression and sometimes even schizophrenia. The main *causes of these diseases are that people do not use their emotions rather they waste their emotions. They spend their precious emotions on those who do not care for their emotions or does not consider the emotions for them meaningful. In doing so our emotions gets severely hurt.*

When it happens to be so then, it leads to be the cause of various diseases as the above. There is a very simple example that can justify this statement; the couples whom we see in day-to-day life. A boy is in deep love with a girl; here be it pure love or emotional attraction or even bodily affection. After dating the boy for a couple of months if the girl happens to ditch the boy then, he will surely be affected with her decision because may be the girl had planned the breakup much before but for the boy it is a all of a sudden shock which might be very difficult for him to face.

If it is the case of bodily affection then, the boy may only suffer from injured self-respect and will forget the matter in quite some days. If it is the case of emotional attachment then, the boy will suffer from deep emotional pain; he will have to detach himself emotionally from the girl to whom he tightly emotionally bonded. This one is very difficult as both emotional attachment and emotional detachment is painful. And in most of the cases it is seen that the person is unable to take the pain and tries to convince the partner for the come-back in relationship.

The request's result is always a bad end up even if positive or negative in its ways. If the partner agrees the come-back in relationship then, it will not be based on the love for her partner but that she could not deny the request of the her partner to whom she shares a emotional connection in particular. And even if she denies the request then, she does it readily which is the proper showcasing of her ultimate feelings towards him. In the first case both the girl and the boy may suffer from the pain of emotional detachment even being emotionally attached.

In the second case the girl may be relived of the pain because however painful she will able herself to detach emotionally from the boy and not further continue the relationship which will in future breakup as emotions are ambulatory in nature. It is so because none of us can stabilize a particular emotion on a particular person. According to situations and persons our emotions also varies from cases to cases.

Like, we may be very angry with our elder sibling if she does not wills to share her new smart phone with us but at the same time we have to modestly request her for the help in preparation of the science project.

In the first case, that is, if the emotionally attached relationships are continued longer and longer then the bondage's cheek by jowl will increase more and more. The closer attachment, the harder is the detachment. Sometimes it happens that our emotions are not in our control; they become unconscious. We may not be aware of the fact that when we have been emotionally so much attached to a person that a severe pain has to be paid for the detachment. And so happens in this case.

The girl and the boy may be thinking that they are reunited in particular but actually not they but their emotions are reunited more closely with each other. Our emotions always enjoy the company of someone to whom it can connect itself or one with similar emotional thinking. The loneliness after the detachment makes the emotions feel alone; they get habituated of a support of some kind in its behavior and now it is unable to handle itself in the absence of the outside support of some kind.

If it is the case of pure love between couples then the physical body can be detached but this emotion of love never gets detached because love alone is the only emotion that never varies with situations and persons. It is stable as it makes two souls connect together with emotion of love. The glue here is love which has a high melting point; nobody can melt it easily or nobody can melt it if it is impurity free. Where there is love there cannot be other emotions and that is why the presence of love is very essential in our life.

Love is like the white blood cells in our body, the organization which is the (physical) defence mechanism of our body. Love is the emotional defence mechanism of the body. Even if the foreign materials (other emotions like: hatred, anger, sympathy etc.) happens to come in contact with our body love sees to their departure. It can fight against anger, hatred and others. It not only prevents their entry on their arrival but also destroys them so that no impurities can move the stability of emotional organization.

Where our emotions are being applied? Whether it is conditional or unconditional? Whether it is purposeful or purposeless; its stability and instability; all are needed to be known as based on these emotions are to be applied. It should not go waste. There has to be no motive in emotional application except the motive of proper utilization of emotions. Emotional problems can be lessened by the correct applying of emotions at the correct time. Bring love in your daily lifestyle to conquer other changing emotions.

<u>*Updating the emotions*</u>

In the day-to-day busy life the emotional expression is barred by our hectic schedule. Like the example of the daily routine of a small family with the parents and two children. The father is very busy with morning physical exercise and the mother too is busy with the preparation of the lunch box and the children have still not seen the sunshine. After the completion of their daily pre-work morning routine they are ready to go to their workplaces and the children to their respective schools.

Even in the workplaces the men and women are hardly able talk closely to their colleagues except the morning greeting exchange. The entire duration of work means the spending of time in meetings and discussions and dealings with the company. In the afternoon during the lunch hour you see them busy typing in their laptops and peering into different files for information. The pens are never put down by them as if they stop to work the whole world will come to an end. If they shut down their laptops their boss will be displeased with them.

In the school, hardly students begin to talk when the teacher warns them for the sealing of their lips (no doubt that the students should concentrate on studies; the purpose they are there in school, that is, to study; to learn instead of spending the entire schooling hours in chatting with friends). But friends are the only ones to whom we share everything; we are never ashamed or embarrassed to make a clean breast of anything to them; frankness is one of the characteristic of friendship. We can share our family matters, study problems, personal problems and anything that is possible.

And when we are unable to share these problems then, the end result is more excitement in the heat of which they automatically begin to talk in the face of the strict orders of silence by the teacher. Not only exciting news and daily talks are the topics of discussions but there are matters also of grief and agony; these immediately needs to be shared to off one's chest. But the tough and big syllabus restricts the chatting program as they have concentrate in order to cope up with the lessons.

Now see how the family members behave after the returning to their abode. They are very tired meeting the busy deadlines and studies in the workplaces and school respectively. Being fatigue the ultimate thing they want to do is go back to the comforts of the feather bed and have a sweet sleep after the beauty bath and tummy-full dinner. Even if there is some time left they spend it in preparing the presentations; the father and the mother constantly staring on the laptop screen and television screen respectively and the children are busy in finishing their homework and studies.

Is this above routine the routine of life? Are we living just to be rich and literates? Even if the father and mother is earning money by being loyal to their way of work but then, for whom are the money earned? To make the life of them and their children crisis-free is the aim; to make themselves is the motive. But here in this routine where is the happiness? There is no happiness in tiredness and also there is no tiredness in happiness. They both are not complementary and supplementary to each other.

They parents can simply go out with their children to a park near their abode or even play games like badminton, cricket or any other particular outdoor or indoor games preferred by them. In this way there exists happiness which binds and rebinds the bondage and also physical fitness is given value. The children learn to play many sports that they are not aware of. The family members spending time with each other brings about a better understanding, cooperation and partnership among them.

Even if every day the addition of this part in the routine is not possible then, at least once or twice a week it can be done. Studies have shown that children not spending with their parents who are unable to make their leisure free are attracted more to their peer group and addicted to harmful sorts of intakes. The married couple who are not having time to give to each other widens the gap of misunderstanding and distrust between them. The old people's psyche automatically chooses solitude in the absence of the presence of family support.

Spending time with each other; be it between married or unmarried couples, among siblings or friends or in other relationships revives the emotion of love that bonds people into one man. Even doing something special for our family or friends; be it gifting a chocolate to your son or daughter, saying "I love you" to your parents, friends and partner; expressing gratitude to the elders or requesting for the shower of blessings of them on you, lending someone a helping hand or a big hand.

If the emotional spirit in relationships is not revived then, it will destroy all the bonding in it as love is the glue of bondage which if degenerates will not be able to generate life relationship. It is very impossible to regenerate love once degenerates (though love never degenerates, it only gets hidden by external barriers). The revival of love in relationships is to be continued to continue the love and the bonding despite which people are strangers to each other even being physically present in relation.

<u>*Barring the emotions*</u>

As discussed earlier there are different types of emotions and 'love' is the unchanging emotion that binds relationship. But despite the advantages we have be conscious regarding its application in practicality[13]. Sometimes we become so emotional; the love overwhelms which forms an opaque layer on our eyes enabling us to remain blind to such truths and issues of which we indeed have an opposite picture in our mind. We are blinded by the emotions in cases we need to consider the matter carefully.

In a parental relationship, the parents often skip the wrongs of the children excusing for the first time and the second time and so on but here being parents they have the complete responsibility of their children; their bringing up. They even does not will to rectify their lads (scolding is absolutely not the way to correct their mistakes nor is hitting but they should be made understood why are they wrong; what can be bad consequences of the wrongs and how will it affect their lives and that of others).

Practicality and emotions are sometimes incompatible. To be practical in a particular one will have to leave behind his emotions in dealing with the case. However there are certain forms of emotions:

①Practical emotions

②Relative emotions

③Sensible emotions

Practical emotions as it sounds are to be practical in nature. The emotions which enable us to be practical at right moment for the right situation with the right method are called practical emotions. One of the practical emotions is stability. It is highly in need for a successful way ahead. Stability is that emotion which enables us to lay stricken to a particular work and thought in spite of various mental disturbances which makes us pay a deaf ear to the work. It enables to stabilize the mind to a particular location to fulfill that particular work.

For example: think of a teacher who had lost both her sons in a car accident. No doubt that she will be upset and trapped in agony and heart-breakage but as a teacher it is her duty to complete the syllabus on time and conduct revision tests before the commencement of the final examinations which is nearly eighteen months after. If she has a lose mental stability the trap of grief will tighten the grip with her but if a strong mental stability will help her to gradually fight against the grief and come back to her normal lifestyle.

Relative emotions are the ones which relate us to something as the name suggests. The emotions which have the power to quickly detach us from the present happening and attaché to the future happenings or the probable happenings or something that has just happened are called relative emotions. It is incompatible with practical emotions which help us to stick to the present happening and the relative emotions detach us from it. It works away from mental stability.

For example: a child studying in his room is called in his mobile phone by his friend. To know the matter he should pick up the phone but should not engage himself in chatting for hours on some unworthy topic according to that moment. Suppose he talked for nearly twenty minutes and the moment he was going to keep his phone down he was immediately attracted by the view of the social networking icons in it and again continued to update his status and message his friends etc. This is the emotion of excitement which relates him to him mobile.

Sensible emotions as the name suggest are sensible in nature; neither practical nor relative rather an admixture of the both. The emotions which partially detach us from the present happening and partially attach to the future happening are called sensible emotions. They are sensible in nature because they neither annihilate the present situation by diverting mind completely from that or it transfers the whole attention to the anticipated happening thus preventing one's mental stability.

For example: when the child studying his subjects is somewhere also aware of the fact that after finishing his studies he will have to attend on birthday party of his chum is a sensible emotion because it is the combination of practical emotion (stability) and relative emotion (excitement). He is neither showing mindlessness towards his studied, that is, despite the thought of the birthday party he is able to concentrate nor he have forgotten of the birthday party despite the home works and studies.

Be known where to use which emotion and also how to control the emotions.

Take control of your emotions least they control you.

CHAPTER TWO

THE COMPLICATED DECISION

How our hearts are hammered when betrayed! How our mirth is at the peak of everything when it finds pillars of its myth! People step in and out of our lives, some stirs, some breaks us. They say that who will come in our life is on destiny, who will be admissible in our life will be decided by us and who will remain in our life will be administered by our behavior.

Whenever we come across someone and starts being fond of him, just because we are impressed by a characteristic trait of his personality, he is a helping hand for us or we are blind-folded by his ace qualities or that we simply love the person. When our heart is busy dealing with the admixture of feelings, the mind creeps along questioning the pros and corns. Nevertheless, the heart always leaps the cold decree. Hardly one is happy when this is worth it.

We are probably not blessed with prophetic powers and so are unaware of the future modes. The job is to depose doubts and show no concern towards it. Instead, one should abolish over-reflecting on relationships and develop it on faithful and progressive lines. In case it does not yield a good profit then remember it was not possible for you to control it. When it goes contrary then lengthen it to the deathbed.

The difficulty of the person not being a right once shall not stop us from interacting with people. If you are robbed out of station then the same condition is not implacable on your home town too. My mother says that the world is not same in its contents. It differs from region to region. Everybody carries their own particular perspective; they have their own ideas that as aforesaid in this book, creates and recreates a human to the best of bests. Our role is to find out the useful perspective; useful in a way not to selfishly benefit us but that which will selflessly benefit the entire society.

In every human quality there is some the other human born. Exemplifying it, Shubhas Chandra Bose, the former of the Indian National Army and the founder of the Forward Bloc; he is the best to put forward in regard to explaining this theory. On case studying him and his achievements or India's gains, it is seen that he was resigned from the congress chairmanship because his patriotic spirit backed him from serving the foreign view of administration and ruling but later due to his socialist beliefs and revolutionary instinct he rejoined the congress chairmanship against Gandhi's wish.

He had to face irreconcilable mental differences as prickling thorns on his way to a newer society. He believed in the support of some external pillar to lead his ideas. His mind always dreamt of building a socialist society for which he turned to bolder methods of agitation. All his instrumental choices in the battle of free-India were against the constitutional methods of Gandhi and Jawaharlal Nehru in particular. No doubt that Mahatma Gandhi was supreme freedom fighter and battler who played a key role in shaping the independent India; free from British Raj.

But even then, even being aware by the non-revolutionary programs' success of Gandhi and the destination he tended to cover during his era why Bose had to turn down to his instincts? Why did he tightly grasp his mentality? Why he had to prefer to stronger procedures being accurately aware of the heavy cost of a drop of blood his countrymen had to shed? Why "You give me blood, I will give you freedom", became is war-cry. Does not a questions jumps in and out of our mind, was he stone-hearted.

No, he was not but he was rather very smart enough to lay-stricken to his idea of revolution; war revolution. Gandhi was no where wrong in his way of dealing with the circumstances but that is what is said, your idea gives a new man to the society. Think if Bose would have followed Gandhi; his ways and methods then, there would have been born another Gandhi because the very man even being differing morphologically will mentally be same. And every society is created by the mental existence of its people and not by their perfectly or imperfectly showcased outlook.

Subhash Chandra Bose instead of doing so when he put forward his process to reach a solution to the problem then, another personality with a new objective and program had originated. Another alternative of protesting he presented to the society which grew its wings worldwide. We are never short of any new idea; we can always turn to newer ways. Just we need draw up to gather the rays of newness and focus them to give beautiful image. So what we think, that is, the ideas we create also sees to the entry of a person in the life. Be careful with your ideas.

From this example, it is cleared conveniently that every a time the righteous person is not the right one to choose for a particular. We have to adopt different qualities and nature of different people and put them into practice at the righteous time; this is another check ID for an understanding human being. It is actually so because we all cannot think of everything no matter to what extent we have touched spirituality, intelligence, smartness and knowledge and any other quality available inside humane figure.

Otherwise, Aryabhatta would not have limited himself to mathematics and would have imparted his deep discoveries on other fields of human benefit and information also. It is not so that he did not put any efforts in that but everyone is made and send for a specific purpose and basic duty and basic purpose to live the life is to get hard at this purpose. The cardiologists would become gynecologist and dentists would have turned out to be scientists; a rock star will become a dancing star and a painter, a choir.

We should train our brain to be brave enough to defy the thought of selecting the 'righteous' person all the times instead should bent to the necessity of the situation and in accordance to the accessing needed for the proceedings and catch hold of the 'eligible' person. Yes, it should be eligible and not righteous. Even none of us can become completely righteous. Can we? No. we all are humans and have committed some sins in the life. And none of us are fortunate to get all the qualities or else different professions on large scale will disappear.

Eligibility is the right word and preference for the choosing the right option; the righteous person. And that creates a need to build up ourselves towards perfection on a particular track. If so is not done then, we will become a waste; useless because our value speaks of our introduction and our introduction provides us with a space in society and that space gives a recognition in the society and later in the world. We create our value on the basis of our ability towards a particular activity. To lose this ability is to lose the recognition.

Work immensely to make yourself able for something to set it as your flair and further lightening it with your capability as a human being. If you are able to take the proper decision of choosing the appropriate person for the necessary job then, it will be the star introduction of you capabilities and abilities.

Continue your search...the 'righteous' person to choose is difficult for he who lacks in quality and easy for he who wins the qualities.

<u>*Admixture of qualities in a person*</u>

There are different persons with each one's qualities differing from those of others. Every quality in all has some or the other developing essence. God has not gifted us all with all the same qualities because he wanted all of us do something different; to prove ourselves in our chosen respective fields. The qualities are different from each other by their own quality. The qualities come together to give rise to a newer form of quality with rank higher in position and place. People may have the same qualities but the quality of the qualities differ them.

Nowadays the pregnant mothers are subjected to a lot of care and nourishment; heavy works are not allowed to do; there are numerous diet restriction; countless medicines of minerals like iron etc. to keep embryo developing and healthy. During pregnancy the women is unable to do a lot of working rather demands constant rest; actually their health demands constant rest. But on the other end there are bevies of women in villages (even in cities) who despite being pregnant does the household works constantly during the gestation.

There are classes of students. In the same class one student can concentrate to listen everything taught in the class for continuously four consequent periods but in the same class there are also some students who puts their best foot forward in listening and jotting down the notes but gradually as the period continues they reluctantly have turn a deaf ear to the teacher. And some students who cannot at all focus on the listening of the taught lessons are busy playing pranks on the teacher and other students.

The simple crowd of people surrounding us in our day-to-day life is another example of differing qualities. Almost everybody has some or the other source of income, be it a big businessman or renowned industrialist; a cobbler or a priest. It is not mandatory that only moneyed people can be social server because of no shortage of finance nor is it compulsory of the poor and the middle-class to be reluctant in helping a needy person financially rather they can do it more properly being able to understand the similar crisis.

There are people with who is very charitable towards his family members and aged parents but at the same time has no concern for the needy and disabled persons in the locality rather the sight of the bent body is a matter of laughter for them. Some can be purely selfless to the others but some cannot find out any reason for being unselfish in their ways. Many a people have the courage to speak the truth at any cost in any situation but some always shiver from the fear of the consequences after speaking the truth.

The list of the different people and their different qualities is endless. People have to be permitted in our lives at the correct moment based on their particular qualities in the correct ways for the correct cause is very important. More important is the quality of the qualities, that is, what is the depth of a person's quality; what is the extent? Its purity and its method, all that describes the quality of the quality is needed to be known. Only the application of the quality is not involved but the method of application is also counted.

Imagine that a boy has molested a girl and person A and person B has received the news. Both the A and B are against harassment and always agitate for its inhabitation. The only difference that differ the same qualities of both of them is the method of their protest. Person A is a sensible man and quickly took action rescuing the girl from the boy and complaining to the police force on time. But person B is very aggressive and to rescue the girl took immediate action by beating the boy so badly that he died of bleeding on the spot. The boy deserved punishment but not death.

Now again imagine the same case of the girl's molestation by the boy, the news of which has been received by both the person A and person B. person A rescued the girl; helped her only for the purpose of helping; he did not have any other motive but person B has decided some financial dealing with the girl and if anything goes wrong with her then, the testament will be immediately cancelled. Person B did not help out of selflessness but out of greediness for the money. This describes the difference in purity of qualities.

Once again imagine the same case of girl's molestation by the boy whose news have reached the person A and person B. Person B did not have the courage to run after the boy in case he runs away to catch him nor he had any guts in presenting himself in the court as an eye-witness to the entire scene to save the girl from the clutches of the boy. But person A is very courageous and was physically and emotionally ready to support the girl to make her grant justice facing up to the challenging situations. This describes the depth and extent of one's quality.

Not only the qualities of a person defines him; they define him partially and the rest half is defined by the quality of his qualities. Select the person on the basis of the method of application of his qualities.

Qualities define a person but the quality of the qualities selects the person.

CHAPTER THREE

WITHSTANDING COMMENTS "The bars to your dreams will be removed when you remove yourself from the cage of other's sayings."

The people are liable to speak. Nobody can draw back this human right from them. Without any doubt, it doesn't permit them to verbally bully others. When something that doesn't belong to you is forced on you just dust it off. If we're so much irate by the taunts then let's reach the very cause of it. People comment on what they don't believe and all we need to do is to make an effort to have their faith by successfully practically executing it .Your initiation to something strange will be shocking to the society as they aren't accustomed to certain things.. But they say, "Only change is permanent in the world."

Anything is enhanced when accompanied by apposite moment and so don't think ahead of time. Everything has with it nothing except birth and validity. They cannot originate before the desired time nor can they exist even a bit longer than a fixed time.

Changes should always be progressive. When we adapt to a change let it be something beyond the outskirts of the previous one. Let not it beat around the bush. Give a good shake to yourself to get rid of the stiffness and be fragile in your ways. Neither be rigid nor be floppy. Be as modest as violet.

Let your behavior be like the free flowing water whose smoothness can break in the hardest rock. Tense yourself to catch the smoothness of the situation and turn the hard edge to the outer killers of the new world. Comments are those words which are produced from the human brain and are emerged to the outside through our mouth and strikes sharply on our heart thus activating it to gather the stored self-motivation and then react it with hardship.

When this reaction is executed tremendous amount of energy is released from our body which enables us to tear away all the bars and two more particles are produced, namely; experience and self-confidence. Both contain benefiting elements for our development of higher personality. The by-products of this reaction are intelligence, enhancement and honour etc. The products have their own ability in respective grounds. The catalyst used is guidance and the promoter working for this is help or self-help.

A good guidance profits to the yield. Imagine you have to visit your child's school to receive his yearly progress card. And the difficulty is that it is your first visit to the school. You are completely clueless of the classroom your child studies in. Here you will be given two alternatives; either poking all the buildings in the school or to simply request a student or faculty to guide you the direction to the classroom. Now what use either will be to you and how?

Preferring the first available alternative you will eventually surely reach the classroom but only some physical stresses has to be paid, like climbing up and down the stairs and covering the wide diameter of the school walking the distance from a building at one extreme to another at completely another extreme. Your preference to the second option will make things a little easier for you. In this case under the proper guidance of the location you will target to walk to the particular building that contains the classroom.

Now is the promoter. Take the previous example for instance. Even under proper guidance if you will not help yourself at least reach the required building or will not pay a proper ear to the direction of the guide, do you think you will be ever meeting the classroom? Good guidance is advantageous but it is not sufficient to meet your destination. But self-help is the tool to fix your destination. Others will help you like bringing up the taste of pizza like sauce but you have to help yourself like the mixing of proper proportion of ingredients to prepare it.

The products of the reaction are all qualities in one quality. Referring to the same previous example then, when you ask for guidance to any available person your interacting ability gains experience of how to converse some official stranger. On learning this chapter of interaction you are all the very well-versed to speak a particular language; your body language even. And even any incorrect posture or gesture, that will poison your persona even to the tiniest part will anti-poison it.

Self-confidence is a very important factor in self-growth and self-detachment from all negativities. Situation unfortunately arises when it seems all the bad luck of the world has been fallen on us. No words of encouragement reach our ears. We become so blinded of our soul by the shattering circumscribing environment in which we are forcefully inscribed, that we tend to lose strength. But miraculously when we are confident by ourselves then it helps awake a new 'one' among us.

God is the justified creator by profession because his small of the smallest creations evokes the sensation of creativity in all. So is His one creation; a verbal creation, that is, infinite speaking by the rest. It is a representing creation as it enables us to increase our focusing towards victory and source of medicine that confers immunity against the external hawks of comments. The confidence is remains conserved.

4. RESPECT FOR SELF-RESPECT

There are persons who have acquired big fame in their lives and are highly reputed, or actually respected. People who have always chosen a dishonest path and is not worthy of respect is another category. There is a third crowd of men also whose stories are aback. They are undertaking ups and downs in their lives and are considered abominable and are often misunderstood due to unfavorable circumstances. They feel alone and left out. Their hardship many a times results in suicide as nobody in this world can live without respect. It is one of the basic needs. Their heinous condition can be remedied by massive program of self-respect.

Let us exemplify the concept. It is however as easy as ABC to understand. An employ in his office despite being very loyal to his boss and hundred per cent faithful towards his duties wrongfully gets blows of warning and scolding from the boss. He zips his lips as he has no guts to stand by himself and go against his master because he has to shoulder the responsibilities of his entire family. And by arguing he may be fired from his job. Subsequently bores all the harshness even if it was getting on his nerves. But have one ever thought what will be its result. He will feel abashed in front of his colleagues and will start considering his work has an abhorrent. He will lack the strength to cooperate with the industry.

And if the situation frequents his life then he will start feeling depressed, as if no one respects him. If this continues for longer, then he may lose interest in life thereby ending it. If he is up to this then think of his family. Who will look after his aged parents? Who will afford to educate his child? Who will accompany his better half in the rest of the life? Above all, who will be able to console them for their irreconcilable loss? Would not it have been better that he would have spoken for himself instead of accepting the wrong?

He may have lost his reputation in front of his boss and deprived of his job but at least he would not have felt disrespected because if nobody, then at least he himself would have respected him. This is the value of self-respect. It has high value in the regards of the mind and body. Some words in English dictionary which are related to ourselves are not unknown to us. Like commonly and most importantly there are, self-love, self-confidence, self-motivation, self-reliance, self-sacrifice, self-centred etc.

Among all other there is one which ravels out any ratty situation. Self-respect; describes the respect for yourself. From aeon newness has been oncoming in the human psyche spread like one up on. With better technological era humans are also leaping towards progressive emotional era. Though from the earliest there is slow realization for the need of self-respect still we have crossed a long way from there. About a couple of centuries India was under the foreign rule and quite mitigated being slaves in their hand.

But gradually self-caring nature of one and all penetrated out of the thick shell of hesitation and fear. People understood they posses their own authority to govern themselves and their authority; their power symbolizes their self-power and self-control and so the demands of any historical movement or procession or be it a charter continued to harp on only one theme, that is, self-governing institution. Then later they were mentally matured enough to know there freedom on themselves; their quality of self-ruling was no hidden to them.

The foreign rule scratched their inner selves which is the sole existence of self-respect. Directly clearing or indirectly speaking, exemplifying or simply defining, the concept of respect for you; yourself is never to go. We demand respect from the outer society; but are you aware how to pull that towards yourself? Respect is to earn; even self-respect you will have to earn it. If we do not respect ourselves then, how will we expect others to respect us?

One who respects his own self will never even tend to disrespect anyone else. The value of respect will be well-known to him. Do not be selfish misunderstanding it; selfishness will not favour you in difficulty as compared to selflessness. To respect yourself is to understand the extension and limit of your personality, qualities and thoughts, basically the work you do and the work done to you.

Do not be timid to hesitate in respecting yourself. You are first person to rule and care for yourself.

CHAPTER FIVE

FEEL THE BONDAGE "If you do not feel the relationship then, you lack life in it as feelings shape a relationship."

Our mothers are superwomen, waking up early in the morning and loading all works on head from cleaning the house, waking us up, preparing herself to attend on her job to preparing our school meal and also spending time with everyone in the family. But if we do not understand the reason why she does all this, then our relation will be incomplete. She is not paid for this, nor is she personally benefited. The only purpose is that there is no purpose to do these things because that forms our bonding. A relationship is not based on its profits and losses; the mother knows nothing except that she loves her child and that love automatically makes her do all that entire she can.

Our fathers spend their energy and strength and to earn money. Why? They are not profited by it rather they spend the money on our education and on the family needs. Here too, there is no purpose for it. His love lets him serve the family. The teacher spends the entire duration of the period in school by standing. Will they not get their salary if they sit down on the chair specifically and exclusively arranged for them? But they want to have a look of the whole class so that everybody remains attentive.

Our friends are the only ones among all persons in the whole world who understands us and be with us. They did not have to study a subject called 'our mind' to be skilled at knowing us. But they love us so they can conjecture our thoughts. What we need to do is to feel their feelings for us. We will always be abortive to find a reason for their work because it is only the execution of their love. We need to understand it or else we will misunderstand them and lose some precious people in our lives.

Work is worship; to work gives strength throughout life from providing satisfaction to introduction. But if that ever becomes the only motive of our lives then, the lively life will be converted non-lively stone. There is something more in the long run that leads to softening it. Actually there are many ways; a smile, a hand on the shoulder or the head on it, a brief heart-to-heart talk, spending time or be it rubbing the rolling the tears; all are sky-touching in their abilities to touch people's heart.

The reason why these evergreen methods have attained a height among relationships instead of the upcoming methods of presenting a posy of rose; flourishing your lad with the latest available gadget in the market; or be it a precious diamond ring to your hurt wife, is that newer methods are materialistic. They do not bring up the fragrance of the relationship then how will you understand it. Like if you only know your mother is preparing a tummy-full lunch and fail to guess the fragrance of the food then, you will not understand what the item is.

So is in relations, we fail the depth meaning of it. Here in relations you have get the details of it. How will you reach a person without his details? Understand the reason of your relationship. Your relation is at the highest level if you actually fail to find a reason, that is, the bondage is bonded on the basis of purposelessness. Every purpose has a start and so meets an end. If there is any objective basis relation it will surely see it end. With the purpose the relation will also end. If it does not follow a purpose then, it will move on and on and on.

Move on to the second question of your relationship. Who is bonded with you in this relation? Always value your needs, rightly. And your relationship with any person has to be both of you contribution. You may be very confident that, " even if the person does not feel the same strong feeling for me, never mind, I will always continue to adore and care for him." You may right in your thinking but the execution will go curvy. Because you may contribute emotionally but if the other side retreats then, it will be imbalanced and ultimately break.

Conversing; communication is one of the four pillars of one's relationship. No matter how pure and clean and easy your bondage is but it is not more piety and humble than parental relation that has immense depth and immeasurable length with non-ending duration. A mother is expertly talented to palmistry the child's needs; his mind and everything. We are not a match with her. But we can try to bring this purity and gentleness in our relationship by knowing each other. And of course we are not astrologers to getting vision of one's internal.

The best way is to communicate with each other. In doing so we come to know a lot about each other; what is their past incidents? And how it is effecting the present? The inspirations and aspirations; the dream goals; hierarchy of person's importance in life; the future views regarding the relation, etc. now we get a brief outline of her mind and heart and for uncoiling the matter to detail it we have to utilize the second pillar of our relationship, that is, understanding; understanding his consideration; his opinions.

Jumping to the third question, is, are you living or dying in your relationship? Both the conditions have a hell-heaven difference. Sometimes we are fed up with the arguments frequenting our relations; sometimes we actually fight in a way to talk; sometimes the realization comes up that we are not be bonded together, but the strangest thing found in some of these cases is do not walk away from that relation instead just try to avoid it because we are too afraid to confess the break-up. And sometimes we are still puzzled of the decision.

The direct affect is on your partner but. He/she kept on troubling with the painful thoughts of why the person is avoiding? Did I go wrong somewhere? Did he play up with me? And sometimes the questions reach to her also. Like, am I not good-looking enough to be loved? Am I so dull in my ways that nobody can date me? Shall I now be considered inferior to my chums who are thriving and driving with their partners? He/she starts feeling low about him/her. As the person is quite not getting any reason of the breaking up of the dreamt relation with you so her heart is abide to go for unnecessary reasons.

This mental instability can be remedied by gutting to speak the apt reason for the breakage of the bond. And in your confused state, you can take a chance to improve your relation, as said already, talk to your partner and move to the root-cause of the problem and further prevail of problems try to completely move back. There can be another type of confusion when you are strongly bonded with your partner and the third pillar of relation is still on its place but due to external factors you are distracted from your relationship.

Here, silent your mind and understand this matter to the whole lot is in your own hand. Instead of using your relationship as a punching bag use it as your support. Instead of hiding matters to your partner share them and get the necessary advice. You will be relaxed because you might be stretching your days thinking there is nobody to share whose depression is expressed in the relation masking its love and also you feel the relation may meet an end. Trusting your partner means trustingly sharing it with him.

Now sometimes we live the bond. Your love seems innate to you. What you can do to preserve the peacefulness of your relation is to strong the four pillars of your relationship, namely; conversation, understanding, love and very importantly respect. Respect is that pillar which binds the debris of the other three pillars. Respect itself is a way of conversing with people, understanding their point of views and loving them. Even if the other three pillars are strengthened it cannot help stand the fourth one.

Be sure-footed for the stand you take for your relationship. Be aware of the relationship you are entering as for you it must be no very hard to break it but the person the person associated with you is your responsibility and be conscious of the same difficulty he/she will face to overcome from the painful truth in her life. Live your life for loving people and face the questions to check the wrong-goings in the relationship. Let not it break if once made.

CHAPTER SIX

OVERTHINKING- A DISASTER "Mind gets exercised and sharpened as you think but it gets over exercised and blunt as you over-think."

The brain is the second stereoscopic part of the body after eyes. It always wants to penetrate into the depth of everything. There was a student who used to make his place among the ten top rank holders in the class. But the situation right about turned and he failed to make up with his syllabus. He ultimately decided not to write the forthcoming examinations because he feared whether or not he will be able to carry the day.

However it is a total misconception as he is not writing the exams and loosing the seventy to eighty per cent of marks for not getting ninety per cent. Is not this an absurd decision? This is an issue of over thinking on his studies which is seriously affecting his present studies. A compulsive shopper always ends up in loss. He is very conscious of the colour and design. Sometimes the brand that we want is not available in the shop. Sometimes the required category of dress is not there. Sometimes the price is too high. However, this can be an excuse.

But, then think of it, is the brand available illegal to wear other than the one we want or will we be put into garbage if the up-to-date design is not worn. Is the colour we want going to have a blinding beauty than the other colours. Take thing lightly. Let our mind be fragile so that the thoughts can be agile to pass across our brain. Let the things be as slippery as an eel and let not they be resisted in our mind. You are born free and can think freely but do not misuse this freedom.

It is not wrong rather is right to check and recheck your thoughts because they ultimately will shine as actions. But is not it a great confusion to differentiate between rethinking and over thinking? The differentiating example stays in our society itself. Have not you noticed parents who are conscious and over conscious about their children? They are too worried about the bringing up of them. They took great care or I will say excessive care of their children while they are studying late nights.

It has also been shown in many television reality shows how parents force their children to attain the top most rank in the class, be the cost of it late night studies or ailing health or an empty stomach. All costs are ready to be paid. But very unfortunately to say, this stresses immense pressure on students who under this curves their path. A standard 10 girl who was the second rank holder of the class murdered her competitor who was the first rank holder just to obtain the highest position in her pre-board examinations.

Yes, rethinking is born from consciousness. A very simple example; a child is attending on his examinations and is very carefully checking his answer leaflet a couple of minutes before the final bell. Even after the pealing of the bell the invigilator has to snatch away the answer leaflet because he is still frightened whether the answers are correct or not. Though he is a very good and studious student, is not it very strange of him to behave in such a way? The student must have spent the night before sleeplessly murmuring the formulas dozily but yet did not give way.

Was it really necessary? But students make it mandatory. They are tightened with the false concept of losing marks if not studied the minute before the examination. There is another case study; what is the greatest reason for the arguments in relationship[11]? There are issues of distrusting, and it is seen that most of the distrust comes by not that the person caught his/her partner red-handed but just because he/she feels his partner is cheating on him/her. This is because he over thinks on the matter instead of thinking.

He/she did not get any proof to think that his/her partner is dating someone else but it is just a belief that it is not impossible for my partner to cheat on me. Why your mind drives to the world of these types of impossibilities? Other than this you may even think it is (do not insert the word 'not' here) impossible for my partner to cheat on me. And if you do not think, it will be turn out to be a foolishness to do so as you should trust your partner or else better your ability to choose a partner or try to drive the trust in your relationship.

God have given us a creative mind. It has many abilities. And to be thoughtful is one of them. And the other contents of the mind are infinite; smartness and common sense are two of them. As human beings we have travelled far somewhere with the knowledge of applications of logics and scientific inventions and historic discoveries but still we are slaves in the hand of our mind. We cannot control. Whether it is anger or be it happiness, all are overwhelming. We do not rule our mind, our mind rule us.

Our inquisitive mind's application are very wrongful some a times. It is not avoidable that successful scientist made successful discoveries when they took up the consideration on tiny matters and laid great stress on their life-cycles etc. But that is what one should note; the correct application of one's power. In spite of big bang in the world of science by the scientist, there are not a less things remaining to know. Other than putting all efforts on small insensible matters look for the bringing up of the still hidden facts.

Now the common question is, our minds are very adventures as if an experienced thinker himself, so how to halt the thinking when it reach the very margin? However, it is not going to be easy because we are unconscious of at which point our mind is out of control (we realize later) and also what is limitation of thinking? But even then it is not undoable. As it is already told that thoughts are represented by actions and every action sees some consequence.

So if you are careful of what you think because at that moment if you can imagine the future of your thoughts, that is, the consequences of your actions then, you will realize the extent of constitutionality or revolutionary extent. The consequence will limit your thinking. Your thoughts will shiver down not being able to dare to take up the terrible consequences. You can wantonly derive an important lesson from it; as you imagine by your mind then, at some corner leave some space to store some energy for noting the sequence of events.

Very shockingly you will learn how with your increase rate of thought level there is an increase in destructive rate of consequences. But on applying the thoughts correctly there will be an increased rate of constructive power. So think well and to do so imagine perfectly and distinctly of the sequence of consequence either from destructive to constructive or from constructive to destructive.

Think well. Live well.

JOY TO BE PRACTICAL "If you are practical to a situation you understand its meaning, causes and consequences. Without these understanding of a situati

The lad dreams of his future beyond the world. He has many priceless ambitions in his life. The childhood and teenage stretches in imagining it but the real joy comes when he practically fulfill the dreams. Implementing the long-term aims indicates completion of his desire. The infant growing in the mother's womb brings a smile to each one's face. All are over-thrilled to get a sight of it and the noise of its pleasant cry entering our ears. But the laughter comes when the baby is born. A storm of happiness accompanies us when we are about to buy our own house.

A prayer service is conducted. Numerous decorative items are purchased. Furniture, kitchen appliances, television set, a wardrobe and countless other materials are planned to buy. But the happiness expands when we start our living in the new house, when our soul gets connected there, when hundreds of memories are there to remember. The woman is very fond of black roses and is joyous without any limit because she is fortunate to plant a black rose. She eagerly awaits the bud to develop. But the real enjoyment is experienced when the tiny bud turns out be a pretty flower.

The man is tensed due to obesity and wants to cut off his weight to be able-bodied. His imaginative muscular body gives him immense satisfaction but he his overjoyed to see that same figure in the mirror itself. Everyone will prefer to be on an outing to a hill station to seeing its pictures in internet. Its joy we experience to be practical as we live the moment. Your realities are far better than the airy-fairies. One dream to be someone ahead but that someone's doodled hazy image cannot relief him with the same quantity of happiness as in real.

And in all realities there has to be some practicalities; some execution. There is no presence of satisfaction in realities in the absence of practicalities. To satisfy this statement to you, the readers are sure to understand it by exemplification. So even here, the reality of reading is behind the overwhelming goodness of imagining some kind of this thought. And understanding the read one is more satisfying than knowing the fact. However, to satisfy your need of more satisfaction there is one simple example below which every citizen is aware of.

Living in the world of the race of political supremacy, what would you have answered to my question, if I ask you, how will you describe a political leader, it may be the prime minister of India or the president or a member of the parliament or state legislative assemblies or other authoritarian political leaders. Will you describe him by his appearance that about his looks, that he should not be dull and boring instead should be able to carry any dull situation to the peak of merriment?

Or will you get upon his family backgrounds; his parents' occupation; his study life and schooling; his positions and contacts with high dignitaries or your amicability with him/her? You would not define him in such a way. Rather you will directly say that he should be well-trained to execute his duty; there should be faithfulness in his duty and loyalty to the nation. As we will esteem him he too should know to esteem other people; his countrymen or an external whether financially stable or unstable.

And the merit list is longer than the neck of a giraffe. So in the contest of the election you cast your precious votes very happily imagining the candidate you have chosen for acceding to the throne and with the outcome of the results that particular candidate is the one who got chosen. It is certain that your happiness will be stronger than the high sea waves; it will better and better happiness than the previous one when there exist only imagination in your mind of your personally selected candidate.

But then again your happiness will turn towards sadness if the expected candidate of yours who was preferred for the taking up of the authority does not seem to carry out his duty. If there is no execution of the affirmation before the taking up of the seat then, will you face him with the same agog? Probably no, you will not. Because all your expectation was not to see him seating on the chair of higher authority but to see him executing his higher authoritarian powers for the development of the nation.

Your second wish is the binding element for your choice of him. That is, the wish to feel the effective basic profit of the execution of his duty lets you like to see him holding a higher authoritarian rank of the nation. In fact your second wish brings you closer to him and you expect something more and more. It means that you also face absolutely no problems in knowing him to be in the works of many extra-Indian activities like, representing India in many international conferences; have the power to declare war and peace etc.

Driving the wedge of execution divides the happening into two parts; namely, undoing or realities and doing or practicalities. Imagination is the shadow of happiness; reality is the tinge of happiness and practicalities is the sac of happiness. We imagine with the desire to experience the shadow of the happiness and then convert it to the tinge of happiness. But it becomes very difficult to get the sack of happiness from the tinge of it. It is not very easy collecting a sack of wheat to finding a grain of wheat.

Practicality's execution has different aspects in such; the first one is to be responsible to the creation of your work. You will have to initialize the consequences of the work with its execution simultaneously. It will leave a good impression on the persons to judge you. As the working of the plan expands the results will automatically be yielded better as there is a direct connection of the implementation to its resultant. When the execution is to reach a conclusion then, skip the results partially and you may look for its benefit.

To understand this concept let us prefer the previous-most example. The prime minister of India is responsible to a number of responsibilities. Though the national working is divided and subdivided between the higher dignitaries yet the prime minister has to look to the detailed working of the nation. So in the execution of his duty if he fails to produce an effective effect, will he be able to hold the trust of the people anymore? People will then doubt his method of working. He will be no more entrusted by the public.

Take for instance the most recent example; our present prime minister, Shree' Narendra Modi', had sought a ban on the notes of rupees thousand and five hundred and replaced it by the new notes of two-thousand and hundred. His order posed a great financial problem not only to the poor people but also it affected aristocratic families who either have reached that position of richness honestly or dishonestly, but the issue was they were affected. Some are benefited while others are not.

To say it more clearly, the prime minister kept up some of the people's trust while lost some of them. This is because he yielded profitable results to some persons who liked his idea and inspired other people to follow the same order of rules patiently and eventually it will help them but on the other hand, there are persons whose financial credit was threatened and so it was constantly found in social networking videos how people cursed the prime minister for the initiation of this rule expressing their personal financial problems.

The financial agony columns were not unknown fact to the newspaper readers in particular. This example very well describes how yield is needed for the continuation of the execution of work. The prime minister would not have been able to continue the policy until he would have received the willing support of majority of people. Luckily and hopefully he received that otherwise strikes and processions would not have been shocking to the people. Still there were many especially with financial problems who protested against this practice.

The second aspect is the understanding the creation of the work. One is sure to fail in his try of executing a work with the basic understanding of it; the work which needs a detailed understanding for its movement. Taking the previous example once again, say how did the prime minister decide to initiate this policy? If you are finding it very hard to read the prime minister's mind then, let me tell you it is not that hard to do. The prime minister needed to know about the cycle of black money from the hands of the dignitaries to the criminals.

He might have caught the sight of the passing of black money and noticed or experienced poverty in his life. These are the basic understanding for the execution of the work because even if the prime minister is well aware of how to start and further execute this policy and yet unknown of the causes to start the policy then, he will find no reason for its execution. And experience may speak a lot here for one understands something that he has already gone through or suffered in his life.

To get detailed with the understanding is the method to perform the work, that is, the execution of the duty. If the prime minister is kept unknown of the method to ban the notes replacing them by newly designed notes even if he is kept known of the causes and consequences of it then, how will his idea work. In the absence of the method there is zero execution. In the presence of the work there is probable possibility of the execution; to make it more probable it again takes us to the first aspect of execution, that is, responsibility.

The third aspect of execution is one's commitment towards the work. Being responsible is to say the partial part of the first aspect. The commitment also adds to the responsibility. The prime minister without any doubt has had to face a lot of agrees as well as disagrees; some curses he received and at the same time not a less blessings were showered on him. The agreement and blessings are sure to actuate him but think of the situation when it came to tackle the bad remarks by the people; the curses of those who have voted for him.

But the commitment towards his work made him able to withstand the whole lot of comments. He was committed to do the job so he refrained from giving way despite corns peppered with pros. If you are firm and stable-minded then, execution is not difficult for you and there is no a happier happiness and satisfying satisfaction than being practical in your ways.

<u>*Leveling your preferences*</u>

Talking about the quality relief to be practical in all your ways sometimes may land you in trouble. You will have to identify the consequences of the work[15].

Based on the consequences will be the execution of the work.

Let us imagine you have never experienced a life behind the bars of a central jail and once sleeping at night you dreamt of it, and even being experiencing that sought of kristallnacht (the night of broken glasses, you hit upon an idea of experiencing it because it is not a bad idea rather a good one to be practical as it is already said imagination is the shadow of happiness, execution is the tinge of happiness and practicality is the sack of happiness. Do you think it really will be sensible enough?

No, absolutely not. Neither its execution nor its practicality nor its consequences makes a sensible remark. Even if you want to execute the work, that is, plots a plan to make away with a costly diamond set of a lady in the market or to make the punishment harder and longer by duration, raping a girl in the return path of her working centre and later being a homicide of her then, what will be the profits of it. What are you to gain? Even if no gains, there will be complete loss of precious years of life and character of yours.

Not only the bad effects will touch you but you will also tend to poison the life of the person associated with the work, in this case, it is the girl. She may suffer from severe depression and phobia of men community. She may be discouraged lead the life forward anymore. Her family may strike with a severe shock. Even if it is of stealing something the person may incur a great loss. He/she may lose the confidence to carry finance or put on ornaments even if it is a simple imitation.

And more apprehensively, think of your own life; the consequences, it will spoil your future career. Even if you try to better yourself it may or may not work as it takes a lot of effort to change the impression and to put the same in the eyes of family, public etc.(however it is not impossible to change yourself; it is in your own hands; your life is in your own hands. And the public opinion is not a judicial statement associated with your case; it does not forcibly imply on your case; if you want to change yourself then, nothing can distract you).

It will be good if one is able to judge the consequences of the execution but it will be far better if one can judge the consequences of even thinking of the execution which results bad yield. As you know, your actions become the representative of your thoughts and thoughts are automatically converted to actions. It becomes very hard to stop the practicality once it is executed. And it becomes more difficult to stop the execution once thought. Think before something is done. Think of the consequences.

To exemplify it; think of a thief, who is very unsatisfied with the day because, albeit paying his level best efforts he was unsuccessful in stealing even a penny, while returning to his home he found a branded car being parked near the gate of a bungalow. The watch man was busy speaking on the cell phone. So it was a nice and big opportunity for him to steal it. Now at this moment it is completely impossible for him to think of the consequences; and so steals it, that is, executes his work.

And once the car is with him the execution becomes practical; practically he is having the car with him. And in case the owner happens to locate the thief he will neither be able to serve himself by stealing nor even by working hard and earning money because he will be subjected to the confinement of the jail where he will even lose his freedom to walk and run on his will; even to sing and dance; to talk to people; to view the spectacular sights of sunrise and sunset which he might not have missed even being penniless.

Therefore, it is rightly said that once something is thought it is very difficult to bar the execution and once it is executed it is much more difficult to cage the practicality. So we should not only think before we speak but also think before what we do. Our thoughts are the ultimate representatives of our actions and our actions directly relate to our reputation (character in such).

Practicality has a newer life in it. But it is to create life when it follows a noble execution which is the follower of the right thought. And the same life-creative factor turns out to be the deathbed when it follows a dishonest and disastrous path.

CHAPTER EIGHT

MENTAL INDEPENDENCE
"We are born to act by thinking. If other's thoughts are disposed on us the word 'new' will vanish."

Our country has been free from the foreign rule for a century and more. There were number of social reformers who made efforts for the rights of women community and depressed classes. But the most important freedom is freedom of one's thought and not actions. One should be given the right for decision-making. Remember, when our actions are obstructed, then our life is restricted, but when our thoughts are obstructed, our living is restricted. Whether the person is older or younger than you, do not restrict him mentally as he is a human and has full right to think and make decisions for himself.

Even our constitution has framed this right as one of the human right. Do not be afraid if the person will be able to take a proper decision or not, even if it is a child, as we are humans who are fully trained to make a decision. Even if one goes wrong then let it be, as one learns from his own mistakes. Let the person learn to take decisions otherwise he will not be able to take up the responsibility of a humanist nation. Let him make his own plans otherwise he will fail to make up himself as a man of weight.

We are living our own life and so should learn to make our own decision. Every time there will not be someone to guide. We should be able to lead our own selves. If we have the guts to come to this life which is rather challenging at every point of it, then we should better know to live it at our own cost and efforts. Nothing is very easy in life. To fight against the strongest enemy we need the toughest tool and that tool has to be constructed by us.

The history of India is an eye-witness to this fact. In the early days the early men had to suffer many problems; many diseases but yet they kept themselves alive; they conquered hunger; they found shelter; they discovered their clothing design. They did not enjoy the facilities we are having now but yet they did not stay back from enjoying their life. Nature has everything; but the problem is it never serves the plateful of solutions to us rather it asks us to find the reason; the symptoms; the consequences; and also its solution.

They did not have anything to wear but the nature has many clothing options. It is in accordance to our knowledge we discover them. Like, the early men could discover the animal skin as a type of wearing. Later when the human era developed a little more then, people laid the foundation of the trees that provide material to make clothes and with the developing human era there are lot more cloths coming up in the market. At each level our brain increases its capacity to think more and do more.

Initially there were only a piece of simple printed clothes that women wore and did all their household works. Then came up the era of jeans and now the upcoming of high waist paints and ankle jeans and torn jeans that is another category, are forcefully depleting this era. And the Indian stores and shops are flourishing with Indian clothes and shoes whether it is nightwear or party wear, be it summer dresses or winter clothes, whether western dresses or Indian clothes.... all the varieties are available.

And in the availability of numerous variety of clothing one can easily switch to different variety of dresses each and every month. And it is completely based on our choice. The days are gone to remain stuck to only on category of dress due to the vanished shortage of dressing nowadays and better designs of wears. We can choose the party wear weather to wear a gown or a quite off-shoulder one-piece. Before we had to lay stricken only to the lose piece of clothes. Mostly benefited are the married women of India.

Earlier post-marriage dresses were only Saree but now they have a number of alternatives; they can wear jeans, gowns, tops, other Indian religious robes. Earlier it was also very difficult for the women folk to swim cross the river wearing their cultural cloth (albeit it did not pose a problem yet it could have) but now the swimsuits are totally solving the problems. There were problems of wearing during physical workouts but now there are dresses specifically designed for it which are indeed comfortable for the task.

Next coming to eating; we have a very evergreen saying in Hindi, that is, "dil ka rasta pet se hokar jata hai (the way to the heart is through the stomach, if you can make it happy by fulfilling it with sizzling foods then, you can surely win the person's heart). In our homes we may be limited to certain food items which are regional or cultural but cooks say that food has the longest and widest diversion in tastes; in varieties; in combinations and be it natural (raw) or cooked. In other countries people may follow the diet routines and all but it is highly restricted by Indians.

The early men started the journey of eating by natural fruits and raw flesh and vegetables. Then they skipped the choice to the mouth-watering cooked flesh when the raw flesh mistakenly fell on the burning fire. Then slowly and slowly when people led to the development of cylinder gases then, they started preparing their own dishes whether it is vegetarian or non-vegetarian. Weather it is raw or deep fried or shallow fried everything seasons our taste buds. There are combinations of food also.

One television cooking show showed the cooking habits of India, namely, Utsav-The Thalis of India. In this show the cook made efforts to visit different regions of India and select a particular family and requested the family members to make him learn about their eating habits by preparing the food items and presenting them on Indian plates (commonly known as, thalis in India). The show opened my eyes to the wide range of food habits and the capability of ingestion and digestion of the people of India.

The plates that the families presented were so filled as not to allow even fly to align at a corner. And different families prepared different food items according to their culture. This demonstrates the fact that though there are different foods in India still people have personally chosen particular food items in their daily food habits. The irony which indeed unites the people of different parts of India is that they love to change the daily food items with the preparations of other culture. This brings taste and national integrity.

Now come to that aspect of life which remained hidden for ages to the Indians especially to the women community. Even after its emergence it remained far flung from the minds of the Indians especially the western education. But gradually due to the efforts of some social reformers in the earlier era like Raja Rammohan Roy and Jyotibe Phule etc., even girls and people of backward classes took to learning be it oriental or western (what matters is education and not its forms; all teaches us the same).

And now with the passage of time almost the whole India is learning western culture and education. There are different streams open to the youth. They can take up medical science, pure science; they can be biochemist; scientist; head of agricultural department; IPS; IS; the principal; lawyers and the list is not ending. They can freely decide their interest and study in accordance to that. Even financial problems are fortunately solved to a great extent by the support of educational loans.

The mental independence says of the independence of the mind and soul. It is freedom to think and to decide. It is the freedom to walk and not to follow.

If the brain and heart i.e. two most vital human organs are not free to work then the human existence will soon turn to inhuman existence. It will be worse than the British rule in India.

DIVERSITY OF OUR MIND

"Human mind is born to explore, it lives for the execution of its exploration. If it dies then, the world's vocabulary will be l

Man has proved his intellectualization from prehistoric ages. They developed the mouth-seasoning cooked flesh when it fell into fire being rotten. The way they covered them with animal skin, the idea was appreciable. They possessed the capacity to think that if they threaten the wild animals with fire they won't dare to step into the caves. They took efforts to make certain tools to hunt animals conveniently. Nobody in the present age is kept unknown of the invention of computer.

The first generation machine abstracted the entire big room. The second generation reduced its measurements followed by the third and fourth one. Researchers are made for the initialization of robots. Computer however fast and quick cannot match men because man himself developed it. Everyone was gripped with the irrational belief of practicing 'sati' as fortunate, female and western education as an incentive to giving up one's religious faith. Everything changed.

People say time is progressing but actually our mind is progressing. There were and still are many reformers who had and are putting efforts respectively to change the society. How? Because, they thought, they thought of the right, they differentiated the right from the wrong and justice from unjust. They forced their minds to do so and so should we do because all men are gifted with a mind to think. If one stops thinking what he can do or what can be done, then progress will stabilize.

If you stop thinking about your career your intelligence will get halted. If you stop reflecting on yourself you lose your introduction. From ages before or from the creation of human life, humans have thought over a lot of things. Their life is based on their minds actually. Our adventures mind is never tired of travelling all the parameters of the universe. Or else it would have been impossible for the astronauts to think to travel in space and land in other planets and satellites. We have dug our mind into the ground a lot.

Constant researches are done to locate a perfect mining area and the transporting them to the required industry; bettering the transport facilities and more than that we did bent down to shoulder the divine responsibility, that is, the cycle of birth and death, we have bested the sanitation facilities and medical equipments. There are short of beds in many hospitals and patients have to lie down in the corridors. There are some cases in which after delivery of the child the infant gets exchanged with some other parents.

This indicates the sharp rise in epidemic of falling health. This serious condition is an emergency which demands for constant action to be taken. Even then, many surgeries are held in the duration of twenty-four hours and there are numerous patients recovering. This is the age of shocks and surprise, where everyday there is something heart-melting and heart-breaking. As the words indicate some relation to heart, so it is. It strikes directly and straightly to our hearts; like my son eloped with her lover; my younger brother extracted the whole property of mine.

And there are no less heart patients in the world; heart-attack, minor or major, is a common problem to many. And to get clearer, we ourselves create this human cycle just like God; we try to take up His position....We do not maintain a proper internal environment of the body neither nutritionally hence physically nor emotionally. In the earlier days people use to work the household works day and night continuously without getting fatigue. But they were never a victim to so many diseases.

But nowadays people has created a rule of not working to avoid health problems and so they appoint a servant to do the daily activities and we on listening the name of exercising mentally feels physically tired. But are we really very healthy? No, almost in every house the senior citizens have to prefer medication after every meal and badly suffer from joint pains. After reaching in thirty's a person is either affected by diabetes or abnormal blood pressure. Recently, one of my classmates got operated in her head.

See, we create facilities for living and conditions of perishing too.

MEDICAL FACILITIES

BIRTHS

DEATH

LESS

HARDWORK

HEALTH
PROBLEMS
PROLONGED
TREATMENT

The above cycle can be remedied by the following flowchart:
BIRTH
IF WORK= SUCCESSFUL
LET LIFE= WORK;

Oval: BIRTH

Diamond: IF   WORK=
SUCCESSFUL

LIFE= MEANINGFUL;

YES

LIFE= EXPERIENCE FULL;

NO

DEATH

Protecting diversity

No doubt that our mind can think a lot; it can reflect over a wide range of facts; when he thinks he executes and when he executes then, something new facts are discovered. But what exists has both sides of it; advantages and disadvantages. Advantages of the diversity of our thinking power are ample in number but the disadvantages are no less than the former. Slowly and slowly one of the major disadvantages of it that is emerging in this era is completely against humanism and humane qualities.

The horde of robbers is planning new methods of making away with the targeted object and they are extending their targets to expensive and more expensive things. The class of student is uniting themselves in a wrong way. The students are discovering new methods of copying and cheating in the examination hall. The men community is trying up to various methods of harassing women community. The invention of smart phones is an important landmark in technological history but many persons are putting it into negative use.

The thinking diversity has different forms of it:
①Positive thinking
②Intermediate thinking
③Negative thinking
④Natural thinking

Positive thinking has two parts: positive evil thinking and positive good thinking. Albeit both belong to the same category of (positive) thinking yet they are distinctly differing in nature. Suppose a student has not prepared well for the examinations and so has prepared a small chit of paper with the eye to copy from it. He is very confident that he *will successfully do the job without being caught. This is an example of positive evil thinking where a person though with evil intentions is sure to goal the aim.*

Take the example of a boy who works his fingers to the bones to get the first position in the examination. On entering the examination hall he is confident about writing the examination and has faith in God, himself and in his studies. This is one of the cases of positive good thinking where a person with a good intention is very confident of a good result. In humanism the positive good thinking is preferred to positive evil thinking because God has designed human heart and soul with the confidence of achieving the goal that follows a noble path.

Next is intermediate thinking. This is actually the second most phase of thinking and also an important phase as it is during this phase when the human thinking nature is decided by its brain. Take the example of a man who catches the sight of the luxurious supercar and plots a plan to steal it and is quite confident regarding his actions. This is positive evil thinking which leads to the intermediate thinking (voice of the conscience), that is, when the person thinks whether the action he will perform will suit his humane or not.

Likely positive thinking, negative thinking has two parts of it: negative evil thinking and negative good thinking. Suppose a man wants to harass a women has employed a person with some amount of money to do the job on his behalf however he is not very sure whether he will escape punishment or not. This is the example of negative evil thinking where a person is with an evil intention and is not very sure of achieving the goal (the voice of his conscience speaks to prevent him).

Take the example of a man who likes a woman and wants to propose her with a beautiful rose but he is not very confident in expressing his feelings and also not very sure that whether or not the women will positively response to his confession. This is the case of negative good thinking where a person is with a good intention but is too conscious to execute it. However, negative good thinking is preferred to negative evil thinking because however negative the thoughts are, goodness always succeeds evilness.

Talking about the natural thinking, when a person is in a normal state then whatever he thinks is categorized to natural thinking. For example: a person watching a television show all of a sudden is impressed by the dressing sense of the hero and dreams of dressing up in the same way for the bachelor party that night. This thought of the dressing is very casual and normal. The natural thinking has many subdivisions according to the situation and the thought. Two of them are: natural evil thinking and natural good thinking.

The natural thought which follows the path of qualities relating to humanism are called natural good thinking. And to the contrast, the thoughts that walk on inhuman paths are referred to as natural evil thinking.

Thinking is not only an act of life but it is a part of life as it is transformed into actions.

<u>*Lack of diversity*</u>

Actions are the representatives of your thoughts.

'The cases of murders and suicides are the widely spread rumours these days'.

The above statement implies on all of us who are totally lacking in emotions. We are neither aware of ourselves nor of else ones. The totally narrow mind is open only to the person being and the rest of the world is left far behind.

People murdering each other are a clear-cut example showing how and to which extent our mind is narrowly shaped (we ourselves are the shapers of our mind. It is not because of the surrounding or company but it is the result of how we want it to be). They cannot open their minds to other ways of tackling the issues with the person murdered; they are unable to expand their thinking. Their minds are limited to the only alternative of murder. This is so because they can hardly think of peaceful means of settlement.

Similarly a person cannot think of any option other than suicide because to their narrow mind no other method of dealing with the problem is available; they do not make efforts to extend the reach of thinking.

How lack of diversity affects can be understood by the following two examples:

• Marriage issues

Fights/arguments

Divorce

Children unsettlement

Court cases

Enmity between families/Enmity between family members

Tensions and stresses

Social problems

• 54 •

Outside emotional support

Family expansion

More complicated court cases

More complicated family situations

Problems with kids of both husbands/wives

Settlement problem

Financial crisis (high fees of advocate)

Mental disturbances

Killing of oneself/other
In this case both the persons (husband and wife) lack the understanding between themselves and also the maturity to solve the problem by various couple-like romantic and practical ways like, communication, trusting, understanding, loving etc.
②The problem with a student:

First rank holder of first terminal

Second rank holder of second terminal

Trying to be the first rank holder

Second rank holder in third terminal

Loses hopes

• 56 •

Did not work hard

Pass marks in fourth terminal

Anguish and frustration

Gave way

Failed

Depression

Abnormal behavior

• 57 •

Psychiatric treatment

Wastage of time

Difficult revival
In this case the student who is the first rank holder of the class faces depression because of loss of that rank once in life. He/she indeed gave way and did not even think to try. He/she did not think that even if not the first rank but at least he/she can bag the second or some other rank instead of failing if tried to do better.
'So live. Live for something so that you can do anything.'

CALMNESS- A SCHOLARSHIP "The power of calmness is when you are calm internally the entire external environment automatically becomes calm."

Let us meet a new scholarship now. It is not completely new but quite evergreen. Have you ever questioned to yourself, what is calmness? Am I calm? Or what will I gain being calm? I am guessing you probably will not give a positive reply to the question. It is so because all of us find it very challenging to be calm in this world of cries of agony and frustration. We never even find it necessary to set ourselves free from all the deadlines to meet. The hectic schedule grasps us just as tiger catch holds of its prey.

Calmness is not a difficult task, nor is a long procedure. It is as quick as lightening. We just need to have its understanding. When you are angry, do not try to avoid it, as it is not abnormal for a normal human being. First step is to get the reason. As you are ready with the reason immediately find its solution. If you are angry with a person, then try to explain him the location of his fault. Or else if you yourself are responsible then instead of regretting better repent your mistake in any available way.

If your anger rages on a specific matter, inhale and exhale longer for sometime so that your mind starts coordinating properly with your body. Discuss the heat of the matter with the specified person. Get the corrections done and the advices needed and you are ready with it fully rectified. Similarly there are many trifle matters which you need to handle on your own. Talking about its advantages, it undoubtedly leads to proper completion of work with zero resistance. Moreover you will feel relaxed.

You will gain the knowledge that you might have missed to take as an advice. Prospects are gained, and suspects lost. The only examination you will have to pass is to control yourself at the very situation when you are angry and the rest will be automatically done. Now talking about the effects of calmness, there are many, namely, peace of mind; peace in the heart; purity of the soul; and cleanliness of the surrounding.

<u>*Peace of mind-*</u>

When you are able to calm yourself in midst of all airheads and hasty situation, it is called peace of mind. For example: when a student comments badly on a teacher then, mostly it is seen that the teacher scolds or punishes the child. But have one ever thought weather the child is really improving in doing so; weather the scolds are at all effecting him in any way. The mentality of the student is affected in another way. He/she seals his/her lips for the time being and finds another opportunity to verbally harass the teacher.

The mentality is affected so wrongly because for them the scolding seems a useless talk. The root of the problem is that they are not aware that they are doing a wrong act and there chums do not understand that they are backing the wrong horse or mainly they do not understand why is it wrong to do what they are up to. And so they feel they have been uselessly scolded which develops a contempt for the teachers; in the face of all bad consequences they are ready to mitigate their desire for revenge at any cost.

In this case if the teacher possess peace of mind i.e. in the midst of all negatives if she/he is able to calm herself/himself then, she/he will reach up to the root of the problem and as she/he is there then, immediately the idea to make them understand in a mild and moderate language of why are they wrong will hit her/his mind. And as we know everyone loves to be respected[10]so they will surely catch their wrong foot and rectify it in the possible ways. It will not affect them but effect to better them. They will not feel comfortable to disrespect the one who respects them despite all bad.

<u>*Peace in the heart*</u>

We cannot live peacefully if we lack peacefulness by heart. If we can grasp the optimism in our heart tightly against all pessimism then, it works to reduce the negativities in our heart. Heart is the biological as well as emotional essential organ to keep a person alive. Doctors have already remarked that if a person cannot be positive to be alive the medicines can hardly cure their illness. Medicines are supplementary access but the head helping hand is our heart which if emotionally alive then, physically also alive.

<u>*Purity of the soul*</u>

It is very true that positivity is born in our heart and also dies in the same cradle as the negative notions gains ground. But no positivity can stir the heart unless there are pure and sensible thoughts within the soul. You are recognized by your heart and your heart is recognized by your soul. If your soul is polluted your heart's purity is disturbed which is automatically outshone in your thoughts, actions and behavior. Reflect on your souls i.e. what you feel internally about the world; about its happenings and its beings, it will help you know yourself better.

<u>*Cleanliness of the surrounding*</u>

One of the greatest personalities, Swami Vivekananda said that if we do not belong to a company then, we should not be found in that company. The words are indeed very reflective in nature. We often say that we are affected by the surrounding but then, why to live in a surrounding that does not suits you? A singer cannot be excused simply because of disturbance in his/her throat because he/she had the cooling bites of ice cream the night before.